Homemade Soaps for Beginners

The Ultimate Natural and Organic Soap Making Guide

Janet Brooks

This book is dedicated to my wonderful husband Jack who has always encouraged me to follow my passions without fear or judgment.

Copyright Act of 1976, the scanning, uploading and electronic sharing of any part of this book without the explicit written consent or permission of the publisher constitutes unlawful piracy and the theft of intellectual property.

If you would like to use material or content from this book (other than for review purposes), prior written permission must be obtained from the publisher.

You can contact the publishing company at admin@speedypublishing.com. Thank you for not infringing on the author's rights.

Speedy Publishing LLC (c) 2014
40 E. Main St., #1156
Newark, DE 19711
www.speedypublishing.co

Ordering Information:
Quantity sales; Special discounts are available on quantity purchases by corporations, associations, and others. For details, contact the "Special Sales Department" at the address above.

This is a reprint book.

Manufactured in the United States of America

Table of Contents

Publisher's Notes i

Chapter 1: The History Of Soap 1

Chapter 2: What Does Soap Consist Of? . 13

Chapter 3: The Variances Of Homemade And Industrial Made Soap 24

Chapter 4: The Methods Used To Make Soap At Home 29

Chapter 5: Safety Is First And Foremost . 41

Chapter 6: What You Need To Get Started Making Soap 44

Chapter 7: Saponification Charts To Assist In Making Soap 48

Chapter 8: How To Use Scents And Colors In Your Soap 103

Chapter 9: Soap Recipes For Beginners . 113

CHAPTER 10: CONCLUSION 152

MEET THE AUTHOR 153

Publisher's Notes

Disclaimer

This publication is intended to provide helpful and informative material. It is not intended to diagnose, treat, cure, or prevent any health problem or condition, nor is intended to replace the advice of a physician. No action should be taken solely on the contents of this book. Always consult your physician or qualified health-care professional on any matters regarding your health and before adopting any suggestions in this book or drawing inferences from it.

The author and publisher specifically disclaim all responsibility for any liability, loss or risk, personal or otherwise, which is incurred as a consequence, directly or indirectly, from the use or application of any contents of this book.

Any and all product names referenced within this book are the trademarks of their respective owners. None of these owners have sponsored, authorized, endorsed, or approved this book.

Always read all information provided by the manufacturers' product labels before using their products. The author and publisher are not responsible for claims made by manufacturers.

Chapter 1: The History Of Soap

When we think of soap, visions of bars of little squares pop up in our heads that we use to clean our bodies with. Since the beginning of time, man used plants literally to keep himself clean. He would do things like break off leaves or use the seeds and scrub his body with them. The earliest man always lived near a water source as water is the source of life. It is a fact that people in early times in general were not as clean as our standards of cleanliness stand today (they were also smellier). The truth is they probably didn't notice it either because everyone smelled the same.

Even now in certain cultures cleanliness is not the same as what we consider it to be. If you go to France the majority of people do not use deodorant under their arms. People learn to adjust to smells. Cases in point, take pet owners who kiss their stinky pets, but don't notice.

It is acknowledged that the Babylonians were making soap around 2800 BC. What the Babylonians used as soap in the period of the rein of Nabondus (556-539 BC) was soap composite consisting of uhulu or ashes, cypress oil and sesame seed oil for washing the stones for the servant girls. A Babylonian clay tablet dating back to approximately 2200 was found with the formula of soap consisting of water, alkali, and cassia oil.

The Ebers Papyrus, dating to ancient Egypt 1550 BC indicates that the ancient Egyptians bathed regularly and combined animal and vegetable oil with alkaline salts to create a soap-like substance. They also mentioned that a soap-like substance was used in the preparation of wool for weaving.

Soap was known to the Phoenicians also dating back to around 600 BC. These early references to what would now be known to be soap, was used in relation to cleansing textile fibers in preparation of wool and cotton to be woven into cloth.

As far as tangible evidence of making "soap" to what we know as soap dates back to ancient Rome. Pliny the Roman historian described soap being made from goats tallow and causticized wood ashes. During those times soap was made by boiling the tallow or vegetable oil with alkali containing wood ashes. He also noted that salt was added to make the soap hard. This was a very costly item in those days, and combined with negative social attitudes of the day about cleanliness, was a luxury afforded for the rich up until the 18th century in most cases. The ruins in Pompeii include a soap factory complete with finished bars of soap.

Despite the fact that the Romans and Greeks were known for their public baths, soap was not used. To clean one's body the Greeks, and then later the Romans would rub olive oil on their bodies mixed with sand and then clean themselves that way. After the skin was cleaned in that fashion they would use a salve of herbs to rub on the skin. Zosimos of Panoplies 300 AD describes soap and soap making.

It is found that throughout history herbs were added to water baths for cleansing purposes. Cleopatra attributed her "beauty" to bathing in mare's milk. During the early century of the Common Era "Soap" was used by physicians in the treatment of disease. In the 2nd century Galen a physician would recommend bathing with soap for certain skin conditions. He describes lye made soap and prescribed it for washing away impurities from the body and cloths. Soap for personal hygiene and cleanliness became popular in Rome during the later centuries of the Roman Empire.

The word "sapo" which is Latin, first appears in a document entitled "Pliny the Elders Historia Naturalis" which details the making of soap from tallow and ashes but its use was for hair pomade not bathing. As the Romans and Celtic cultures interacted more and more historically, many credit the Celts with actually perfecting the making of soap and using it for washing and bathing as a common standard. The truth is both of these peoples were inventive and it so happens they both discovered it independently of one another. While the Romans started using soap in public bathing by the 3rd century AD in the big cities the small villages used an olive oil, sand and strigil method to clean themselves. The fact of the matter is the Celts may have been washing their faces with soap long before the Romans trekked over the Italian Alps.

There is a legend as to the first origins of who made soap. The legend goes that the first soap was discovered by women washing their clothes along the Tiber River along the bottom of the Sapo Hill. Legend has it that the women found their clothes were cleaner with far less effort in that area. The ashes and the grease of animals from the sacrificial fires of the temples situated on the top of Sapo Hill mixed with the rain, made "soap" which ran down the slope in the streams of rain water giving the women a wash day bonus. You can see at a glance saponification, the chemical name for the soap making reaction, bears the name of that hill in Rome long ago.

After the fall of the Roman Empire in the West, there was little soap making being done during the Dark Ages. However in the Byzantine Empire the remnants of the Roman Empire in Eastern Mediterranean Area coupled with the Expansion of the Muslim World had the Arab world making and using soap at that time. From the beginning of the 7th Century from the Nablus or West Bank, Kufa/Iraq and Basra/Iraq peoples made and used soap. They even added advances to the making of soap. In those areas, soap was perfumed and colored. Some of the soap sold in that area of the world was liquid and some was solid. They even had a special shaving soap.

The Persian Muslim Chemist Al-Razi wrote a manuscript at that time on recipes for true soap. Recently a manuscript was discovered from the 13th century which detailed the recipes of soap making by the Arab world at that time. Soap was sold for 3 Dirhams or 0.3 Dinars a piece in 981 AD. Some of the details included taking sesame oil, a splash of potash, some lime and alkali and them mixed together and boiled. After boiled it was poured in to molds where it cooled and hardened. This soap was considered pleasant to use and was imported by the Europeans from the Arab lands at that time in the Mediterranean. It was bought and shipped across the Alps to Northern Europe by means of Italy.

In around the 8th Century, soap making was revived in Italy and Spain as well. Soap makers were members of a guild. There were indeed public bath houses in

Europe during the middle ages called stews. There, patrons were given large wooden tubs and a bar of soap to use to bathe with. The rich patrons had their own private tubs. It was later in the medieval period that baths grew out of favor. The authorities of the time closed the public baths because they felt it spread the plague. During the latter part of the medieval times, and into the Renaissance, people moved away from bathing to keep clean. It was at that time that heavy scents masked the body odors instead of soap and water.

By the 13th century France also became involved in making soap in Europe. In the 14th Century, England took up the making of soap as well. Soaps that were produced in southern Europe; namely Italy, Spain and the Southern Ports of France (which made Marseilles and Castle soaps) made soap from olive oil. The soap from these areas were higher in quality than those from England and Northern France.

The North of Europe was not able to get olive oil and had to make their soaps from tallow (animal fat). They also resorted to oil from fish to make soap. Soap that was made from poor quality animal fats and oils was suitable for laundry and textiles but not for bathing. Since the soaps from Southern Europe were far superior, an active trade ensued with soap being exported and imported from Southern Europe.

In France by the Second half of the 15th Century soap was manufactured in a semi industrialized way from a few prime centers that supplied the rest of France. London was the center of soap production at that time as well. By the 16th century finer soaps were produced in Europe based around using vegetable oils like olive as opposed to animal fat. Of these soaps, castile soap which is and was all vegetable-based, was the oldest of the white soaps of Italy.

As the early settlers made their way to the new world they brought soap with them. They relied on making soap themselves from the animal fat and what was available, than waiting for it to arrive from Europe. Despite the fact that soap was a valuable commodity in the new world, bathing for cleanliness still was not common until between the late 17th and 18th centuries.

It wasn't until the industrial revolution that soap making was conducted as an industry so to speak. It was William Gossage who first produced low priced good quality soap in 1850 in Lancaster England. American manufacturer Benjamin T. Babbitt introduced marketing innovations that included sale of bar soap and distribution of product samples. William Hesketh Lever and his brother, James, bought a small soap works in Warrington in 1885 and founded what is still one of the largest soap businesses, now called Unilever. These soap businesses were among the first to employ large scale advertising campaigns.

Today in the industrialized parts of the world with a better understanding of personal hygiene, soap is used as a defender against pathogenic microorganisms that are found on the body.

Chapter 2: What Does Soap Consist Of?

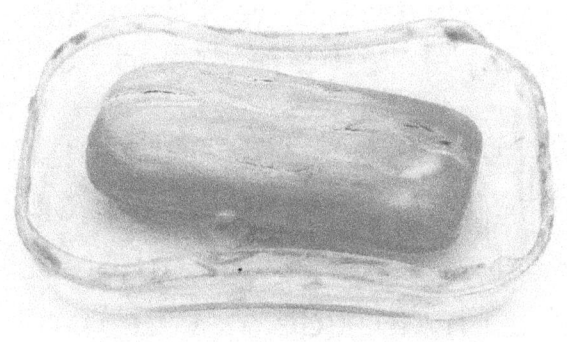

In chemical terms soap is a salt of alkali metal such as sodium or potassium with a mixture of what are called fatty carboxylic acids. Soap becomes "soap" as the result of a chemical reaction called "Saponification". In simple terms saponification is the name for the chemical reaction between an acid and a base that forms into soap.

There are different ways to make soap. You also have the choice of different types of acid to choose from to act with a base in order for the saponification to happen. There is one rule however; the base must always have one ion of hydroxide. For this reason many people use Lye which is composed of one sodium ion and one hydroxide ion.

You can note that the sodium ion does not take part in the saponification process. For this reason other bases like potassium hydroxide may be used. This is because of the fact that potassium hydroxide also has one ion of hydroxide for saponification. Potassium Hydroxide is widely used as a popular base for those who make liquid soap. Your acid can range from a variety of things for example, olive oil, coconut oil or tallow to name a few.

Each acid has its own unique combination of triglycerides. Triglycerides are compounds that are made up of three fatty acids attached to a single molecule of glycerol. Each triglyceride combines with the base differently. The amount of base required to effectively interact with a triglyceride depends on the chemical makeup of the acid. What happens is when you mix the proper proportions of the base to the acid a reaction occurs; saponification. The triglyceride in the acid releases the single glycerol molecule which transforms to skin enriching glycerin when released. When the glycerol molecule is released it allows the fatty acids to combine with the hydroxide ions to form with the base into soap.

So the process of making soap has two chemical reactions that occur. The first one is the glycerol which turns into glycerin. Second is the acid and the base from a salt which is soap.

The early or traditional types of soaps bear little or no resemblance to many of the soap on the market today. By definition of what soap is; most on the market today are detergents which are made from petroleum based products. Those that contain products found in nature are many times radically changed in high energy processes.

Here is a traditional recipe for soap from colonial times. Soaps of those days were made in three basic steps:

1. Making of a Wood Ash Lye
2. Rendering of cleaning the fats
3. Mixing the fats and lye solution together; and then boiling the mixture into soap

Here is the Recipe for Making the Lye First

The first step in making the soap is making a liquid called "potash" known commonly as lye.

The lye solution was obtained by placing wood ashes in a bottomless barrel set on a stone slab with a groove and a lip carved in it. The stone in turn rested on a pile of rocks. To prevent the ashes from getting in the solution a layer of straw and small sticks was placed in the barrel then the ashes were put on top. The lye was produced by slowly pouring water over the ashes until a brownish liquid oozed out the bottom of the barrel. This solution of potash lye was collected by allowing it to flow into the groove around the stone slab and dripped down into a clay vessel at the lip of the groove. Some colonists used an ash hopper for the making of lye instead of the barrel method. The ash hopper was kept in a shed to protect the ashes from being leached unintentionally by rain fall. Ashes were added periodically and water was poured at intervals to ensure a continuous supply of lye. The lye dripped into a collecting vessel located beneath the hopper.

Now the Fats are Prepared

The preparation of the fats or grease to be used in forming the soap was the next step. This consisted of cleaning the fats and grease of all other impurities contained in them.

The cleaning of fats is called rendering and is the smelliest part of the soap making operation. Animal fat, when removed from the animals during butchering, must be rendered before soap of any satisfactory quality can be made from it. This rendering removes all meat tissues that still remain in the fat sections. Fat obtained from cattle is called tallow while fat obtained from pigs is called lard.

If soap was being made from grease saved from cooking fires, it was also rendered to remove all impurities that may have collected in it. Cooking grease being saved over a period of time without the benefits of refrigeration usually became rancid. This cleaning step was very important to make the grease sweeter. It would result in a better smelling soap. The soap made from rancid fats or grease would work just as well as soap made from sweet and clean fats but not be as pleasant to have around and use.

To render, fats and waste cooking grease were placed in a large kettle and an equal amount of water was added. Then the kettle was placed over the open fire outdoors. Soap making was an outside activity. The smell from rendering the fats was too strong to wish in anyone's house. The mixture of fats and water were boiled until all the fats had melted. After a longer period of boiling to ensure completion of melting the fats; the fire was stopped and into the kettle was placed another amount of water about equal to the first amount of water. The solution was allowed to cool down and left over night. By the next day the fats had solidified and floated to the top forming a layer of clean fat. All the impurities being not as light as the fat remained in water underneath the fat.

You can observe this today in your own kitchen. When a stew or casserole containing meat has been put in the refrigerator, you can see the next day the same fat layer the colonists got on the top of their rendering kettle.

The Soap Making Can Begin

In another large kettle or pot the fat was placed with the amount of lye solution determined to be the correct amount. This is easier said than done. We will discuss it more later. This pot was placed over a fire again outdoors and boiled. This mixture was boiled until the soap was formed. It was determined that the mixture was soap when the mixture boiled up into a thick frothy mass, and a small amount placed on the tongue caused no noticeable "bite". This boiling process could take up to six to eight hours depending on the amount of the mixture and the strength of the lye.

Making soap with wood ash lye only made soft soap. When the fire was put out and the soap mixture was allowed to cool, the next day revealed a brown jelly like substance that felt slippery to the touch, made foam when mixed with water, and cleaned. This is the soft soap the colonists had done all their hardest and best to produce. The soft soap was then poured into a wooden barrel and ladled out with a wooden dipper when needed. To make hard soap, common salt was thrown in at the end of the boiling. If this was done a hard cake of soap formed in a layer at the top of the pot. As common salt was expensive and hard to get, it was not usually wasted to make hard soap. Common salt was more valuable to give to the livestock and the preserving of foods. Soft soap worked just as well as hard and for these reasons the colonists, making their own soap, did not make hard soap bars.

In towns and cities where there were soap makers making soap for sale, the soap would be converted to the hard soap by the addition of salt. As hard bars it would be easier to store and transport. Hard bars produced by the soap maker were often scented with oils such as lavender, wintergreen, or caraway and were sold as toilet soap to persons living in the cities or towns.

Hard soap was not cut into small bars and wrapped as soap is sold today. Soap made by the soap makers was poured into large wooden frames and removed when cooled and hard.

The amount of soap a customer wanted was cut from the large bar. Soap was sold usually by the pound. Small wrapped bars were not available until the middle of the 19th century.

This technique laid the foundation for soap that we use today. Of course it's not as difficult by any means and the qualities of the ingredients are far superior but the principal of making soap remains the same. The base and the acid have to mix to create the soap.

Chapter 3: The Variances Of Homemade And Industrial Made Soap

One of the main differences between industrial made soap and handmade is the quality of ingredients. The quality and type of ingredients are different than the general industrial soaps. As people are moving away from chemically bombarded things in their lives, they are also moving towards more natural quality soap. If you notice even the commercial soaps are adding what they consider natural ingredients to their products. You will see industrial soaps with Aloe, vanilla and lavender now just like homemade soaps, in an effort to grab the natural oriented consumers.

The main ingredient that makes homemade soap stand out from industrial soap is the fat content. Homemade soap usually contains a higher fat content which makes it more skin friendly than industrial soap. In homemade soap there is an excess of fat used to consume the alkali called "super fatting". With super fatting the glycerin is not removed, leaving a more moisturizing type of soap as opposed to just a soap cleanser. Another factor is by additional processing of the glycerin yields glycerin soap. You have to be careful with homemade soaps and fat because in the old days homemade soap was greasy and left a greasy feel to the skin which was not pleasant. So even though soap is "homemade" the fat content has to be monitored.

Some homemade soapers/soap makers add things like natural emollients such as jojoba oil or Shea butter at the point of saponification where the ingredients homogenize and begin to thicken called at trace. It is added at this point because it is believed that it will escape being included in the saponification process and remain intact especially in the hot process of the making of soap. This is because it has been added after the main oils have saponified and thus remains intact. Super fatting can also be achieved by a process called lye discounting. Lye discounting is where instead of adding extra fats to the mix, less lye is added in the initial saponification process. In both hot and cold soap processing heat may be required for saponification.

The main distinctions between homemade and industrial soaps also include the use of more natural ingredients like jojoba or olive oil. Also the amount of vitamins and oils are trace to non in industrial soap. At home, soap is made by the cold press process. This also lends to the oils and things added in remaining intact.

One thing that both, soap at home or in a factory have in common is the saponification process. They both have to go through the lye or sodium hydroxide and fat interaction to create a soap. That is the only way the soap can occur. In hot soap making process the mixture is heated to 80 to 100 degrees C for the saponification process to occur. What happens is that by the time the process ends 90% of the lye is gone. In some cases all the lye is gone by the end of the process.

The first and foremost difference between homemade and industrial soap is indeed the glycerin content. Glycerin is a clear liquid that absorbs water from the air. This is what keeps skin healthy and soft. In handmade or homemade soap the glycerin is kept during the saponification process. In industrial soaps the glycerin is usually reduced to put into lotions. This is the main thing that makes homemade soap more skin friendly than industrial.

Chapter 4: The Methods Used To Make Soap At Home

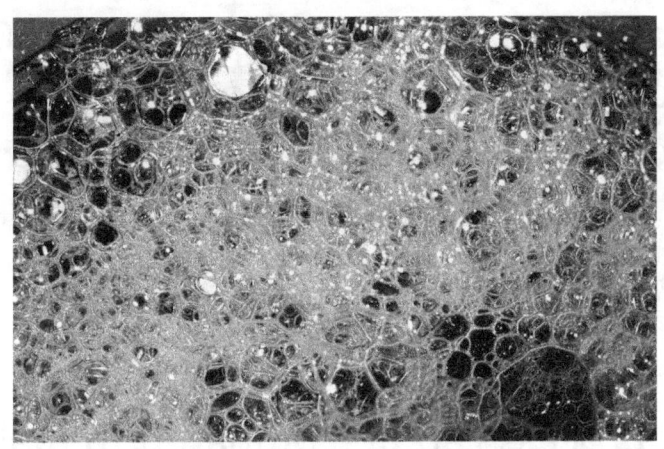

There are 4 different processes you can use to make soap at home. They are:

1. **Melt and Pour**-Melt pre-made blocks of soap and add your own fragrance

2. **Cold Process**(This is the most common)-making soaps from scratch with oil and lye

3. **Hot Process**-soap is actually cooked

4. **Rebatching**-grinding up bars of

soap, adding milk or water and reblending them

Each Method has its pros cons and variations. The majority of homemade soap makers use the Melt and Pour, Cold Process and Rebatching. So for the purposes of this book we will leave out the hot process as an option for making soap at home.

Melt and Pour Soap Process

This process can be compared to making a cake with a cake mix. You don't have full control the same way with the ingredients or recipe customization, but it makes up for it in easiness, convenience and safety.

When you make melt and pour soap, you buy pre made blocks or shavings of uncolored, unscented soap base from craft stores or soap maker suppliers. You can Google the soap maker suppliers if you do not know of a craft store for the soap base.

What you do next is you melt the base soap either in a double boiler on the stove or even the microwave. When the soap is completely melted, you can add in color fragrance or other additives. Once the additions are put in the melted base you pour it into a mold, let it harden, and when it does you got soap!!! It's that simple.

To get started on making melt and pour soap all you need is:

- A clean counter top or work space
- A double boiler or microwave
- A heat resistant bowl for the microwave
- A couple of spoons or whisks
- Melt and pour soap base
- Your fragrances, colors or other additives of your desire
- Something to Mold the soap in (you can buy all kinds of nice molds

online or just use something easy like a silicon muffin pan; this is what I use when I make any soap)

That's all that is needed to make this type of soap. It's fast easy and fun. It's a good project for parents with kids.

Pros of Melt and Pour Technique

- An easy an inexpensive way to make soap
- No need to deal with dangerous lye mixtures
- You don't need a lot of ingredients to start
- Soap is ready to use as soon as it hardens

Cons of Melt and Pour Technique

- No real control of your ingredients
- Melt and Pour is not quite as "natural" as it can be for a homemade soap (this is because it is already manufactured unless you

look for an all-natural base, added chemicals for lather allows for easier melting)
- Your soap is only as good as the base you purchase

Cold Press Soap Process

The first thing you need to make cold pressed soap is a recipe. There are many, many recipes you can choose from. When you get the recipe of your liking you then need to gather all your ingredients, materials that the recipe requires (recipes will follow in later chapters). You want to start by organizing your work space.

The things you need to get started with the cold press method are:

- A flat, uncluttered workspace with a heat source and access to water
- Fat; either vegetable or animal
- A pitcher of lye water
- A soap pot and easily found tools

and equipment
- Fragrance or essential oil
- Natural or synthetic colorant if desired
- A mold to pour the mixture into
- A cool dry place for the soap to cure

Because it takes time to cool; you want to start by making your lye solution first and then put it aside in a safe place. **Lye is a caustic, dangerous chemical. You must handle it with care!!!! It can cause some serious burns.**

When preparing lye you want to have all your ingredients in place before you actually start handling them. Also, you want to use rubber gloves and goggles and keep your skin covered as much as possible. Just as there are variations on making soaps the same is true for lye.

To make a cold pressed soap you heat the oils in a pot until they are 100 degrees. You then slowly and carefully add the lye mixture until it thickens to a trace. A trace is a point of no return in the heat process where the mixture will not separate back into the original lye water and oil.

The way to make sure the mixture is at trace is to test it. You can test it by dipping a spatula or spoon into the mixture and then letting it dribble back into the pot. Some people describe a trace as a little mound of soap that takes a second or two to disappear back into the batch. To be at trace point it does not have to be very thick but it just needs to be mixed well and there should be no streaks of remaining oil visible.

Some soap makers like to pour their mixture into molds at light trace and others prefer a heavy trace where the liquid has thicken a great amount. The trace above is a moderate trace.

When the mixture reaches trace you can then add your fragrances, color and additives to the mixture and then pour it in the molds. Raw soap takes about 24 hours to harden and about 4 weeks to cure for use.

Pros of Cold Press Method

- You are truly making soap from scratch
- You control all the ingredients in the soap
- You can tailor the basic recipe with endless variations

Cons of Cold Press Method

- You have to learn how to work safely with lye
- You need more ingredients and tools to start
- It takes longer to make and more cleanup is involved
- You have to wait several weeks until the soap is ready to use

Re-Batched Soap Process

Making soap the re-batched way is literally taking scraps of already made soap; grating it and then melting it, adding additional colors, fragrances, and any additives you want. It is grated and reprocessed soap. Most soap makers re-batch for three main reasons:

- To fix a mistake on a batch that was already made
- To use delicate or temperamental ingredients that will not survive the initial soap making process.
- To use scraps of soap in a constructive manner

Pros of Re-Batching Soap

- To add specific light and delicate fragrances
- Fragrances and oils that are prone to seizing
- Colors that are extremely ph sensitive

- Additives that are affected by the lye and turn brown (like lavender buds)
- Additives that will melt by the time the soap gels (like jojoba beads)

Cons of Re-Batching Soap

- It never completely melts; becomes a gloppy mass that is thick and glossy. You have to press it many times to get it into the molds
- Air bubbles get trapped in the soaps surface making it hard to get a smooth finish look
- If you already made a cold press batch and want to repress it for adding specifics that can't withstand the cold press process its extra work
- the soap ends up looking rustic or primitive

It's a good idea to test out colors and fragrances with soap. You can feasibly make a 5 pound batch of unscented soap; and re batch it into 5, one pound batches each with distinct colors and scents. It's also very useful if you made a mistake on a cold pressed batch. You may not have the right color or smell or the additives don't look right or feel right in the soap. In this case re batching is very useful.

When the soap is grated or chunked up its put either in a double boiler or crock pot, just as you would use a pot for the cold press method.

You have to use a liquid to melt the soap in. Some people use water, (I used to add dry milk to the water). You can also use cows, goats, or coconut milk. It makes the re-batch mix smoother than just water. You want to pour in just enough liquid to wet the soap. There are re-batching recipes also to help you with amounts.

Generally the longer soap has been left in a mold determines the amount of liquid you want to use to re batch it. If the soap is about a week old you can start with 2 to 3 ounces of liquid per pound of grated soap. Start with 2 ounces; if it's not wet enough add another.

Chapter 5: Safety Is First And Foremost

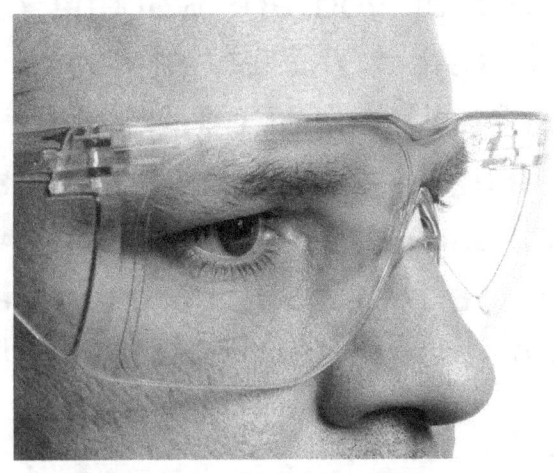

You should follow a few safety precautions when making your soap.

The first thing in being safe is being organized. You want to organize all of the equipment and ingredients you are going to use to make your soap. You do not want to run into another room because you forgot a piece of equipment or ingredient when you start your process.

It is important that the utensils and equipment you use is are in good working condition (nothing broken) and clean. You also want to make sure that the surface that you are working on is protected. Protect the counter and the floor with newspaper or other protective materials like old towels. Old vinyl table cloths and shower curtains work well also. It's important to have a bottle of vinegar on hand. Vinegar neutralizes spills.

If you work with someone else or a child educate them that soap making can be dangerous before you start. Label the pitchers and spoons carefully. **Never leave lye, lye water or uncured soap unattended. That can mean an accident waiting to happen!!!**

Make sure you understand how to make lye safely. Lye is a potentially dangerous chemical with nasty injuries. It can be used quite safely as long as you respect it. You don't have to fear lye just know what you are doing. Before you actually use lye, if this is your first time go over the instructions/recipe as how to make lye water first. Understand what you are doing before you start.

You must wear proper eye and hand protection while making soap. Soap is caustic for the first 24 hours; keep your hands and eyes protected through the whole soap making process.

It's important to work undistracted; do not work around small children or pets. Secure your pets and small children from coming into the work space. **Never leave the pots or oils on the heat unattended.**

When you make soap it's extremely important to work in an organized methodical fashion. Take your time. Accidents and errors occur when you rush.

Chapter 6: What You Need To Get Started Making Soap

Here is a List of things you need to make your soap:

1. An accurate scale *(Ideally one that measures to 1/10th of an ounce)* for measuring **everything** including the oils, lye, fragrance, additives and even your water
2. A 2-3 quart heat-resistant plastic or stainless steel pitcher with lid for mixing up your lye solution (I prefer clear plastic) - clearly labeled

"danger lye"

3. A large stainless steel or plastic spoon for stirring the lye solution
4. If you're making small batches (2-3 lbs) of soap, you can start with a large Pyrex pitcher to mix everything in. If you want to make bigger batches, you'll need an 8-12 quart stainless steel pot (Your "Soap Pot") with lid for melting your oils and blending the soap
5. Another 2-3 quart glass or plastic bowl or pitcher *(Large Pyrex pitchers work great)* or a large bowl for measuring and holding your liquid oils before you add them to the soap pot
6. An accurate, quick reading thermometer for monitoring the temperature of the lye solution and the melted oils
7. Stainless steel measuring spoons to measure the fragrance or essential oils, colorants and/or additives

8. A few small beakers, ramekins or measuring cups to hold the fragrance/essential oils, colorants, separated soap, and/or additives before you add them to the soap pot
9. A large stainless steel or plastic ladle to ladle out a bit of the raw soap to blend colorants
10. A Stick blender to blend the oils with the lye mixture and start the saponification process
11. A soap mold to pour your raw soap into (many different options here - from a commercial soap mold to yogurt cups, a shoe box, or Tupperware container). Basically any leak-proof container made of plastic, glass or stainless steel. Wood or cardboard molds can be used too if they are first lined with freezer paper
12. A couple of rubber spatulas to scrape any last bits of soap out of

the pot
13. Paper towels or dishcloths to wipe up the inevitable spill
14. Some kind of protective covering for your counters and floor
15. Rubber gloves to protect your hands and goggles for your eyes

The more experienced you become at soap making the more you will start to fine tune your equipment and tools to suit your needs. Each soapers has their own unique technique in making soap; the same goes for the equipment they use. But regardless of soap style these are the basics in some form everyone who makes soap uses.

Chapter 7: Saponification Charts To Assist In Making Soap

As we have seen from the earlier chapters the saponification process has to occur in order to make soap. A saponification chart is one where the amount of lye is calculated against the fat depending on the type of fat it is. It's called the SAP. This lets you know how much of both to use in a recipe. In general terms all recipes are based on weight, not volume. This is why you need a good scale to weigh both the lye base and the fat of your choice. Here are some charts to help you with the process. Knowing the exact amount of caustic soda or sodium hydroxide to be added to the different oils or fats that you may use is important (because if you add too much, it could burn your skin). If you add too little, your soap will contain excess fat which will cause your soap to go rancid.

Chart 1

In this chart the SAP value is expressed as number of mg KOH (sodium Hydroxide) required to saponify 1 gram of oil/fat. Most soapers will prefer to calculate the amounts themselves in ounces. You will see these values listed on charts a lot of times in converted decimal amounts. These are the actual SAP values as opposed to the true SAP values. To convert SAP values into converted values ready to work with in ounces you need to:

For Solid Soap/ (NaOH): Divide the SAP Value by 1422.9803

For Liquid Soap/ (KOH): Divide the SAP Value by 1010.316

In this chart the lye is a little lye heavy and the oil on the lower end.

Lipids	SAP	NaOH	KOH (oz.)	Name
Acai Berry Oil	186-200	0.136	0.191	Euterpe oleracea Fruit Oil
Almond Butter, Sweet	90-140	0.098	0.139	Prunus amygdalus dulcis (Sweet Almond) Oil
Almond Oil, Sweet	190-200	0.137	0.193	Prunus amygdalus dulcis (Sweet Almond) Oil
Almond Oil Sweet Organic	190-200	0.137	0.193	Prunus amygdalus dulcis (Sweet Almond) Oil

Aloe Vera Butter	240 - 260	0.176	0.247	Cocos Nucifera (Coconut) Oil and Aloe Barbadensis Leaf Extract
Aloe Vera Oil	185 - 200	0.135	0.191	Glycine Soja (Soybean) Oil (and) Aloe Barbadensis Leaf Extract
Andiroba Oil Refined	165 - 210	0.132	0.186	Carapa Guianenis(Andiroba)Nut Oil
Apricot Kernel Butter	130 - 145	0.97	0.1361	Prunus Armeniacae

				(Apricot) Kernel Oil
Apricot Kernel Oil	185 - 195	0.134	0.188	Prunus Armeniacae (Apricot) Kernel Oil
Apricot Kernel Oil Organic	185 - 195	0.134	0.188	Prunus Armeniacae (Apricot) Kernel Oil
Argan Oil, Virgin Organic	180 - 200	0.134	0.188	Argania Spinosa (Argan) Oil
Argan Oil Deodorized	180 - 200	0.134	0.188	Argania Spinosa (Argan) Nut Oil
Argon	180	0.134	0.188	Argania

Oil Virgin Organic	- 200			Spinosa (Argan) Oil
Avocado Butter	177 - 198	0.132	0.186	Hydrogenated Persea gratissima (Avocado) Seed Oil
Avocado Oil	177 - 198	0.132	0.186	Persea gratissima (Avocado) Oil
Avocado Oil, Organic	177 - 198	0.132	0.186	Persea gratissima (Avocado) Oil
Babassu Oil	245 - 256	0.176	0.248	Orbignya oleifera (Babassu) Seed Oil

Baobab Oil	190-220	0.143	0.202	Adansonia digitata (Baobab) Seed Oil
Beeswax Pellets, White Filtered	89-103	.067	0.95	Beeswax
Black Cumin Seed Oil	185-205	0.137	0.193	Nigella sativa (Black Cumin) Seed Oil
Black Raspberry Seed Oil	184-191	0.132	0.186	Rubus Occidentalis
Blackcurrant Oil	185-195	0.134	0.188	Ribes nigrum (Blackcurrant) Fruit Oil
Borage	175	0.130	0.184	Borago

Oil	-196			officinalis (Borage) Seed Oil
Brazil Nut Oil	192-202	0.138	0.195	Bertholletia excelsa (Brazil) Nut Oil
Broccoli Seed Oil	172	0.121	0.170	Brassica oleracea italica (Broccoli) Seed Oil
Buriti Oil	185-240	0.149	0.210	Mauritia flexuosa (Buriti) Fruit Oil
Calendula Oil	190	0.134	0.188	Glycine Soya (Soybean) Oil (and) Calendula

				officinalis (Flower) Extract (and) Tocopherol
Camelina Oil	185-197	0.132	0.1859	Camelina sativa (Camelina) Seed Oil
Camellia Oil	185-197	0.134	0.189	Camellia oleifera (Camellia) Seed Oil
Camellia Oil, Organic	185-197	0.134	0.189	Camellia oleifera (Camellia) Seed Oil
Candelilla Wax Pellets	43-65	0.038	0.053	Candelilla (Euphorbia cerifera) Wax

Carnauba Wax Flakes	78-95	0.061	0.086	Carnauba (Copernicia cerifera) Wax
Carrot Oil	190	0.134	0.188	Glycine Soja (Soybean) Oil (and) Daucus carota sativa (Carrot) Root Extract (and) Tocopherol
Castor Oil	175-187	0.127	0.179	Ricinus communis (Castor) Seed Oil
Cherry	182	0.135	0.190	Prunus

Kernel Oil	- 202			avium (Cherry) Kernel Oil
Cocoa Butter (deoderized)	188 - 200	0.136	0.192	Theobroma cacao (Cocoa) Seed Butter Deodorized
Cocoa Butter, Pure, Prime Pressed	188 - 200	0.136	0.192	Theobroma cacao (Cocoa) Seed Butter
Cocoa Butter, Ultra Refined	188 - 200	0.136	0.192	Theobroma cacao (Cocoa) Seed Butter
Coconut Oil (76A)	250 - 264	0.178	0.252	Cocos nucifera (Coconut

				) Oil
Coconut Oil, Organic	250 - 264	0.178	0.252	Cocos Nucifera (Coconut) Oil
Coffee Bean Butter	175 - 200	0.132	0.186	Coffea arabica Seed Oil (and) Hydrogenated Vegetable Oil
Cranberry Seed Oil	192	0.135	0.190	Vaccinium Macrocarpon (Cranberry) Seed Oil
Cucumber Seed Oil	180 - 190	0.130	0.183	
Cupuac	188	0.136	0.191	Theobro

u Butter, Refined	- 198			ma grandiflorum (Cupuacu) Butter
Emu Oil, AEA Certified Fully Refined Grade A	185 - 200	0.135	0.191	Emu Oil
Emu Oil, AEA Certified Fully Refined Ultra	185 - 200	0.135	0.191	Emu Oil
Emu Oil, Clear AEA Certified	185 - 200	0.135	0.191	Emu Oil

Evening Primrose Oil	175 - 196	0.130	0.184	Oenothera biennis (Evening Primrose) Oil
Evening Primrose Oil, Organic	175 - 196	0.130	0.184	Oenothera biennis (Evening Primrose) Oil
Flax Seed Oil	188 - 196	0.135	0.190	Linum usitatissimum (Linseed) Seed Oil
Flax Seed Oil, Organic	188 - 196	0.135	0.190	Linum usitatissimum (Linseed) Seed Oil
Fractionated Coconut Oil	325 - 340	0.234	0.239	Caprylic/ Capric Triglyceride

Grape Seed Oil	185-200	0.134	0.188	Vitis vinifera (Grape) Seed Oil
Grape Seed Oil, Chardonnay	176-194	0.130	0.183	Vitis vinifera (Grape) Seed Oil
Grape Seed Oil Organic	185-200	0.135	0.191	Vitis vinifera (Grape) Seed Oil
Grape Seed Oil, Riesling	185-200	0.135	0.191	Vitis vinifera (Grape) Seed Oil
Green Coffee Oil	170-220	0.137	0.193	Coffea arabica (Green Coffee) Oil
Hazelnut Oil	180-	0.134	0.188	Corylus american

	200			a (Hazel) Seed Oil
Hemp Seed Oil	190 - 195	0.135	0.191	Cannabis sativa (Hemp) Seed Oil
Hemp Seed Butter	175 - 200	0.132	0.186	Cannabis sativa Seed Oil (and) Hydrogenated Vegetable Oil
Hemp Seed Oil, Organic	190 - 195	0.135	0.191	Cannabis sativa (Hemp) Seed Oil
Illipe Butter	188 - 200	0.136	0.192	Shorea stenoptera (Illipe) Seed Butter
Jojoba,	90-	0.064	0.091	Simmond

Clear	93			sia chinensis (Jojoba) Seed Oil
Jojoba, Natural	91-93	0.065	0.091	Simmondsia chinensis (Jojoba) Seed Oil
Jojoba, Organic Clear	90-93	0.064	0.091	immondsia chinensis (Jojoba) Seed Oil
Jojoba, Organic Golden	90-93	0.064	0.091	Simmondsia chinensis (Jojoba) Seed Oil
Karanja Oil	185	0.130	0.183	Pongamia Glabra (Karanja) Seed Oil
Kokum	187	0.134	0.188	Garcinia

Butter	-193			indica (Kokum) Seed Butter
Kukui Nut	190-195	0.135	0.191	Aleurites moluccana (Kukui) Nut Oil
Lanolin Oil	90-110	.070	.099	Lanolin Oil
Macadamia Nut Butter	175-200	0.132	0.186	Macadamia ternifolia Seed Oil (and) Hydrogenated Vegetable Oil
Macadamia Nut Oil	190-200	0.137	0.193	Macadamia (Macadamia ternifolia)

					Seed Oil
Mango Oil (Olein)	180 - 195	0.132	0.186		Mangifera indica (Mango) Seed Oil
Manketti Oil	190 - 205	0.139	0.195		Ricinodendron rautanenii (Manketti) Oil
Maracuja Oil (Passion Flower Oil)	185 - 205	0.137	0.193		Passiflora incanata (Passion Flower) Seed Oil
Marula Oil	188 - 196	0.135	0.190		Sclerocarya birrea (Marula) Kernel Oil
Marula Oil, Organic	188 - 196	0.135	0.190		Sclerocarya Birrea (Marula)

				Oil
Meadowfoam Oil	169	0.119	0.167	Limnanthes alba (Meadow foam) Seed Oil
Monoi de Tahiti Oil, Unscented	250 - 264	0.178	0.252	Cocos Nucifera (Coconut) Oil (and) Gardenia Tahitensis
Moringa Oil	190 - 205	0.139	0.195	Moringa (Moringa oleifera) Oil
Neem Oil, Certified Lead Free	175 - 205	0.134	0.188	Azadirachtin indica (Neem) Oil
Nutmeg		0.117	0.165	Myristic

Butter				fragrans
Olive Oil	194 - 196	0.133	0.188	Olea europaea (Olive) Fruit Oil
Olive Butter	125 - 150	0.088	0.124	Olea europea (Olive) Seed Oil (and) Hydrogenated Vegetable Oil
Olive Oil, Extra Virgin	184 - 196	0.133	0.188	Olea europaea (Olive) Fruit Oil
Organic Red Raspberry Seed Oil	188	0.132	0.186	Rubus Idaeus (Red Raspberry) Seed Oil

Palm Kernel Oil	220	0.155	0.218	Elaeis guineensis (Palm) Kernel Oil
Palm Oil	190 - 205	0.139	0.195	Elaeis guineensis (Palm) Oil
Palm Oil, Organic	190 - 205	0.139	0.195	Elaeis guineensis (Palm) Oil
Papaya Oil	180 - 200	0.134	0.188	Carica papaya (Papaya) Seed Oil
Passion Flower Oil	185 - 205	0.137	0.193	Passiflora incarnata (Passionfruit) Oil
Peach Kernel Oil	193	0.136	0.191	Prunus persica (Peach)

				Kernel Oil
Pecan Oil	191	0.135	0.190	Algooquian pacaan (Pecan) Nut Oil
Pequi Oil	190 - 200	0.137	0.193	Caryocar braziliensis (Pequi) Seed Oil
Perilla Oil	185 - 200	0.135	0.191	Perilla ocymoides (Perilla) Seed Oil
Pistachio Nut Butter	175 - 200	0.132	0.186	Pistacia Vera Seed Oil (and) Hydrogenated Vegetable Oil
Pomace	189.	0.133	0.188	Olea

Olive Oil	7			europaea (Olive) Fruit Oil
Poppy Seed Oil	196	0.138	0.194	Oleum Papaveris (Poppy) Seed Oil
Pumpkin Seed Oil	187-195	0.134	0.189	Cucurbita pepo (Pumpkin) Seed Oil
Pumpkin Seed Oil, Organic	187-195	0.134	0.189	Cucurbita pepo (Pumpkin) Seed Oil
Red Raspberry Seed Oil	188	0.132	0.186	Rubus Idaeus (Red Raspberry) Seed Oil
Rice Bran Oil	190	0.133	0.188	Oryza sativa (Rice)

					Bran Oil
Rice Bran Oil, CP	180 - 190	0.129	0.181	Oryza sativa (Rice) Bran Oil
Roasted Coffee Oil	175 - 195	0.130	0.183	Coffea Arabica
Rosehips Oil	185 - 193	0.133	0.187	Rosa canina (Rosehip) Fruit Oil
Rosehips Seed Oil, Organic	185 - 193	0.133	0.187	Rosa canina (Rosehip) Fruit Oil
Safflower Oil High Linoleic	185 - 198	0.135	0.190	Carthamus tinctorius (Safflower) Seed Oil
Seabuckthorn	130 -	0.116	0.163	Hippophae

Oil	200			rhamnoides (Seabuckthorn) Oil
Sesame Oil	186-199	0.135	0.191	Sesamum indicum (Sesame) Seed Oil
Sesame Oil, 100% Organic	186-199	0.135	0.191	Sesamum indicum (Sesame) Seed Oil
Shea Butter	170-190	0.126	0.178	Butyrospermum parkii (Shea Butter) Fruit
Shea Butter, Organic Crushed &	170-190	0.126	0.178	Butyrospermum parkii (Shea Butter)

Refined				Fruit
Shea Oil	170-195	0.128	0.181	Butyrospermum parkii (Shea) Seed Oil
Soybean Oil	190	0.134	0.188	Glycine soja (Soybean) Oil
Soybean Oil, Organic	190	0.134	0.188	Glycine soja (Soybean) Oil
Stearic Acid	207 - 211	0.147	0.207	Stearic Acid
Sunflower Oil, High Oleic	191	0.134	0.189	Helianthus annuus (Sunflower) Oil
Sunflower Seed Oil,	185 - 198	0.134	0.189	Helianthus annuus (Sunflow

Organic				er) Seed Oil
Tamanu (Foraha Oil)	185 - 235	0.148	0.208	Calophyllum inophyllum (Tamanu) Oil
Virgin Coconut Cream Oil	248 - 265	0.180	0.254	Cocos nucifera (Virgin Coconut) Oil
Walnut Oil	190 - 197	0.136	0.192	Juglans regia (Walnut) Seed Oil
Watermelon Seed Oil	188 - 195	0.135	0.190	Citrullus Lanatus (Watermelon) Seed Oil
Wheatgerm Oil	180 -	0.135	0.190	Triticum vilgare

	200			(Wheat) Germ Oil
Yangu (Cape Chestnut) Oil	192.2	0.135	0.190	Calodendrum capense (Yangu) Oil

OTHER LIPIDS	SAP	NAOH (oz.)	KOH (oz.)
Beef Tallow		0.140	0.196
Canola Oil		0.123	0.173
Corn Oil		0.135	0.190
Cotton Seed Oil		0.137	0.192
Mustard Oil		0.122	0.172
Niger-Seed Oil		0.135	0.1890
Peanut Oil		0.135	0.190
Rapeseed Oil		0.124	0.175
Shortening, Vegetable		0.136	0.1904

Chart 2

When you use or design a soap recipe you want to consider the fat to lye ratio so the end product is mild for the skin. This chart has a 5% fat cushion. As you become more adept at making soap you may have your own ratio variations as well. With this chart if you want to add a little bit of super fatting oil at the end, you can also do it with the lighter numbers even though the super fatting element is already taken into consideration.

To use this chart you take the amount of fat you intend to use in a particular recipe (in ounces) and multiply it by the decimal number assigned to that type of fat. The result will be the amount of lye you need in ounces. You can round the numbers up to finish your calculations, but it is suggested to wait and round up all the fat amounts and then add them first for a particular recipe to determine fat to lye ratios. If you are combining fats; you add the results of the calculations and then see how close it comes to the standard 12 ounces of lye. For many soapers the ideal recipe will use 12 ounces of lye. You can then adjust the amounts accordingly. Also 1/4 of the fat content you use to make soap should be one that is hard at room temperature. Of course this is not written in stone, it's a guideline. Another rule of thumb is the water you use is approximately 1/3 of the total weight of the fats. This means you add up the weight of the fats and oils and divide that number by three for the ounces of water to use. Many soapers like to have a small cushion of extra fat for a mild product and strive for about 5% to 8%.

Saponification Numbers for Lye (Sodium Hydroxide)

Milder Column with a 5% Discount

OIL	OLD	MILDER
Almond Oil (Sweet)	.136	.129
Apricot Kernel Oil	.135	.128
Avocado Oil	.133	.126
Babassu Oil	.175	.166
Bear Tallow	.139	.132
Beef Tallow	.140	.133
Bees Wax (White)	.069	.069*
Brazil Nut Oil	.175	.166
Butterfat, Cow	.1619	.154
Butterfat, Goat	.1672	.159
Camellia Oil	.1362	.129
Canola Oil	.134	.129
Castor Oil	.1286	.125*

Chicken Fat	.1389	.132
Cocoa Butter	.137	.130
Coconut Oil	.190	.1805
Cod Liver Oil	.1326	.126
Corn Oil	.136	.129
Cottonseed Oil	.1386	.132
Crisco/Veg. Shortening	.136	.129
Flaxseed Oil	.1345	.128
Grapeseed Oil	.1265	.120
Hazelnut Oil	.1356	.129
Hemp Seed Oil	.1345	.128
Java Cotton Oil	.137	.130
JoJoba Oil	.069	.066
Karite Butter (Shea)	.128	.122
Kukui Nut Oil	.135	.128

Lanolin (Wool Fat)	.0741	.070
Lard	.138	.131
Macadamia Oil	.139	.132
Maize Oil	.136	.129
Mink Oil	.140	.133
Mustard Oil	.124	.118
Neat's Foot Oil	.136	.129
Neem Oil	.136	.132
Niger Seed Oil	.135	.129
Nutmeg Butter	.116	.110
Olive Oil	.134	.128
Olive Pomace Oil		.126
Palm Butter	.156	.148
Palm Kernel Oil	.156	.148
Palm Oil	.141	.134

Peanut Oil	.136	.129
Perilla Oil	.137	.130
Poppyseed Oil	.138	.131
Pumpkinseed Oil	.133	.126
Rapeseed Oil	.134	.129*
Rice Bran Oil	.128	.122
Ricinus Oil (Castor)	.129	.125*
Safflower Oil	.136	.129
Sesame Seed Oil	.133	.126
Shea Butter	.128	.122
Shortening (Vegetable)	.136	.129
Soybean Oil	.135	.128
Sunflower Seed	.134	.1275

Oil		
Tallow, Deer (Venison)	.138	.131
Tallow, Bear	.139	.132
Tallow, Beef	.141	.134
Tallow Sheep (Mutton)	.138	.131
Tallow, Vegetable	.135	.128
Tallow, Goat	.138	.131
Walnut Oil	.135	.129
Wheatgerm Oil	.131	.124
Wool Fat (Lanolin)	.074	.070

* Number higher than 5% difference because it works better than dropping down too much.

To make soap it takes a given amount of

lye to completely saponify an ounce of a certain fat with no excess fat or lye left over. This is what the numbers are based on. If you want a cushion of "extra" fat so that the soap is milder you build it by having 5% more fat in the recipe than you would have lye, to saponify it. So to make a milder soap you need 5% excess of fat. This is done by either adding on more fat or reducing the amount of lye in a recipe ratio. Regardless of which way you decide to go by, either adding fat or decreasing the amount of lye, the end result has to be a 5% difference (some soapers want a higher percentage with the fat being higher). Once you figure out how much lye it takes to get a perfect saponification with no extra fat or lye; then you take that number and multiply it by .95 or 95%. This will then give you the amount of lye you need for that extra cushion. Here is an example of how it is done:

Say you have a recipe of 12 ounces that would perfectly saponify the fats in your soap; you would then multiply **12 oz. x .95 = 11.4 oz. of lye.**

If use **11.4 oz.** for that recipe you would end up with a 5% discount of extra fat for that recipe. This also helps to protect you against errors with measurements. You can still do a little bit more super fatting if you wish but be careful if you get carried away the soap with be soft or spongy. The MMS lye calculator is nice because it gives you measurements in three areas (although the one that says "proceed with caution" would be fine if you are totally accurate with your measurements).

What makes things a little more complicated is the fact that there is more than one SAP chart out there in the world to choose from. You can super fat in a number of ways it's not a magic phenomenon. If the saponification was completed that soon, we could use the soap as soon as it got hard without aging it (like when you cook it). If your super fatting agents have special qualities you want to retain (like vitamin E.) then it might be worth adding them at the end when there's not as much free lye present, but for the other oils, I just add them up front and do the recipe with a 5% discount built in. Super fatting in that case is optional.

Chart 3

This chart shows amounts for both Sodium Hydroxide (lye) and Potassium Hydroxide (used for making soft or liquid soaps)

Use the following saponification chart or table for making soap by multiplying the number of grams of oil or fats by the figure stated and this will give you the exact amount of sodium hydroxide to saponify it. For example, if you are going to use 150 g of sunflower oil or olive oil, multiply 150 x 0.134 which will give you 20.1 grams. You can round up or down your numbers accordingly, and therefore I would only add 20 grams of sodium hydroxide or caustic soda to the sunflower or olive oil to get the correct balance and to saponify your soap.

If you are working in ounces, follow the same process, using the figures on the saponification chart. The amount of sodium hydroxide you will need will be expressed in ounces. Therefore 16 oz. of sunflower or olive oil will be multiplied by 0.134 resulting in 2.1 oz. of sodium hydroxide. Add 2 oz. of caustic soda to your soap.

If you are using more than one type of oil in a single **soap recipe**, do the above step for each oil used on the saponification chart and then total your results together to get the total amount of lye needed. By using the saponification chart learning how to make soap can suddenly become a whole lot easier!

OIL	SODIUM HYDROXIDE NaOH	POTASSIUM HYDROXIDE KOH
Apricot Kernel	0.1350	0.1890
Arachis	0.1360	0.1904
Avocado	0.1330	0.1862
Babassu, Brazil Nut	0.1750	0.2450
Beef Hoof	0.1410	0.1974
Beeswax, White	0.0690	0.0966
Brazil Nut	0.1750	0.2450
Butterfat, Cow	0.1619	0.2266
Butterfat,	0.1672	0.2340

Goat		
Canola	0.1240	0.1736
Castor	0.1286	0.1800
Chicken Fat	0.1389	0.1944
Chinese Bean	0.1350	0.1890
Cocoa Butter	0.1370	0.1918
Coconut	0.1900	0.2660
Cod-Liver	0.1326	0.1856
Coffee-seed	0.1300	0.1820
Colza	0.1240	0.1736
Corn	0.1360	0.1904
Cottonseed	0.1386	0.1940
Earthnut	0.1360	0.1904
Flaxseed	0.1357	0.1899
Florence, aka Olive	0.1357	0.1876

Gigely Tree	0.1330	0.1862
Goose Fat	0.1369	0.1916
Grapeseed	0.1265	0.1771
Hazelnut	0.1356	0.1898
Hemp Seed	0.1345	0.1883
Java Cotton	0.1370	0.1918
Jojoba	0.0690	0.0966
Kapok	0.1370	0.1918
Karite Butter Shea	0.1280	0.1792
Katchung	0.1360	0.1904
Kukui Nut	0.1350	0.1890
Lanolin	0.0714	0.1037
Lard	0.0741	0.1932
Linseed	0.1357	0.1899
Loccu	0.1340	0.1876

Macadamia	0.1390	0.1946
Maize	0.1360	0.1904
Mink	0.1400	0.1960
Mustard	0.1241	0.1737
Neat's Foot	0.1359	0.1902
Niger-seed	0.1355	0.1897
Nutmeg Butter	0.1160	0.1624
Olium Olivate	0.1340	0.1876
Olive	0.1340	0.1876
Palm Butter	0.1560	0.2184
Palm Kernel	0.1560	0.2184
Palm	0.1410	0.1974
Peanut	0.1360	0.1904
Perilla	0.1369	0.1916
Poppyseed	0.1386	0.1936

Pumpkinseed	0.1331	0.1863
Ramic	0.1240	0.1736
Rape	0.1240	0.1736
Rice Bran	0.1280	0.1792
Ricinus	0.1286	0.1800
Safflower	0.1360	0.1904
Sesame Seed	0.1330	0.1862
Shea Butter	0.1280	0.1792
Shortening (veg.)	0.1360	0.1904
Soybean	0.1350	0.1890
Sunflower Seed	0.1430	0.1876
Sweet Oil	0.1340	0.1876
Tallow, Bear	0.1390	0.1946
Tallow, Beef	0.1405	0.1967
Tallow,	0.1245	0.1883

Chinese Vegetable		
Tallow, Deer	0.1379	0.1930
Tallow, Goat	0.1383	0.1936
Tallow, Sheep	0.1383	0.1936
Teal/Teel/Til	0.1330	0.1862
Theobroma	0.1370	0.1918
Tung	0.1377	0.1927
Walnut	0.1353	0.1834
Wheatgerm	0.1310	0.1834

Chart 4

This chart is a variation on the first one.

This one is measured in weight not volume. It is suggested when using conversion to always use weight measurements such as pounds, ounces or grams. Always measure the fats and lye the same way. For example if you use ounces for fat you must use ounces for the lye. As you know by now water is also needed for the saponification process. Using too much water may result in soft soap bars that require extra drying time. In order to determine the correct amount of water to use; first determine the amount of lye you need to use for your recipe. To calculate the correct amount of water; first determine the amount of lye you are going to use then divide the lye amount by 0.3; then subtract that amount from the lye and that will give you your amount of water to use.

1. (Amount of Lye) ÷ 0.3 = (Total Weight of Lye Water Solution)

2. (T(Amount of Fat) × (Saponification Value of the Fat) = (Amount of Lye)

3. Total Weight of Lye Water Solution) – (Amount of Lye) = (Amount of Water)

Here is an example:

For example, to make just over 2 pounds of olive oil soap, measure 32 ounces of olive oil and 4.33 ounces of lye because 32 ounces of olive oil × 0.1353, which is the saponification value for olive oil, = 4.33 ounces of lye. Next, to calculate the correct amount of water: 4.33 ounces of lye ÷ 0.3 = 14.43, which will be the total weight of the solution (lye and water). Subtract the weight of the lye from the solution (14.43 − 4.33) to get the weight of just the water, which equals 10.10 ounces of water.

Remember, after weighing the lye (sodium hydroxide) and water, always add the lye to the water; never add water to the lye.

FAT OR OIL	LYE / SODIUM HYDROXIDE NaOH	CAUSTIC POTASH / POTASSIUM HYDROXIDE KOH
Almond Oil	0.1367	0.1925
Aloe Vera Butter	0.1788	0.2518
Aloe Vera Oil	0.1421	0.2001
Apricot Kernel Oil	0.1378	0.1941
Avocado Butter	0.1339	0.1886
Avocado Oil	0.1337	0.1883
Babassu Nut Oil	0.1749	0.2463
Beeswax(animal)	0.0689	0.0970
Borage Oil	0.1339	0.1886
Candelilla Wax	0.0322	0.0454

Canola Oil	0.1328	0.1870
Canola Oil, High Oleic Acid	0.1330	0.1873
Castor Bean Oil	0.1286	0.1811
Cherry Kernel Oil	0.1389	0.1956
Chicken Fat(animal)	0.1356	0.1910
Cocoa Butter	0.1378	0.1941
Coconut Oil, Refined at 76 degrees	0.1910	0.2690
Coconut Oil Hydrogenated at 92 degrees	0.1910	0.2690
Coconut Oil, Fractionated/Saturated	0.2321	0.3269
Copha Vegetable	0.1910	0.2690

Shortening		
Corn Oil	0.1368	0.1927
Crisco Vegetable Shortening	0.1369	0.1928
Emu Oil (animal)	0.1377	0.1939
Evening Primrose Oil	0.1362	0.1918
Flaxseed Oil	0.1358	0.1913
Goat Fat (animal)	0.1382	0.1946
Goose Fat (animal)	0.1349	0.1900
Grapeseed Oil	0.1321	0.1861
Hazelnut Oil	0.1369	0.1928
Hempseed Oil	0.1359	0.1914
Jojoba Seed Oil	0.0695	0.0979
Jojoba Seed Liquid Wax	0.0695	0.0979

Kremelta® Vegetable Shortening	0.1910	0.2690
Kukui Nut Oil	0.1351	0.1903
Lanolin Animal!	0.0748	0.1054
Lard Animal!	0.1399	0.1970
Linseed Oil	0.1358	0.1959
Macadamia Nut Oil	0.1391	0.1913
Milk Fat Animal!	0.1599	0.2252
Mink Oil Animal!	0.1403	0.1976
Monoï de Tahiti Oil	0.1796	0.2530
Neem Tree Oil	0.1372	0.1932
Olive Oil	0.1353	0.1906
Ostrich Oil Animal!	0.1385	0.1951

Palm Kernel Oil	0.1777	0.2503
Palm Oil	0.1420	0.2000
Peach Kernel Oil	0.1361	0.1917
Pumpkin Seed Oil	0.1389	0.1956
Rapeseed Oil	0.1328	0.1870
Rice Bran Oil	0.1284	0.1808
Safflower Oil, High Linoleic Acid	0.1374	0.1935
Safflower Oil, High Oleic Acid	0.1369	0.1928
Sesame Seed Oil	0.1336	0.1882
Shea Butter	0.1296	0.1825
Soybean Oil	0.1359	0.1914
Soybean Oil, 27.5% Hydrogenated	0.1361	0.1917
Stearic Acid, Animal-Source	0.1413	0.1990

Animal!		
Stearic Acid, Vegetable-Source	0.1411	0.1987
Sunflower Seed Oil	0.1358	0.1913
Sunflower Seed Oil, High Oleic Acid	0.1351	0.1903
Tallow, Beef Animal!	0.1419	0.1999
Tallow, Deer Animal!	0.1382	0.1946
Tallow, Sheep Animal!	0.1384	0.1949
Tamanu Seed Oil	0.1437	0.2024
Tiaré Flower Oil	0.1796	0.2530
Walnut Oil	0.1349	0.1900
Wheat Germ Oil	0.1319	0.1858

These saponification values indicate the amount of lye (sodium hydroxide) or the amount of caustic potash (potassium hydroxide) needed to completely saponify the listed fat using consistent units of weight.

Chapter 8: How To Use Scents And Colors In Your Soap

Scents:

As a general rule of thumb, you will need anywhere from 1.5 to 4 ounces of fragrance or essential oil to scent an 8 pound batch of cold processed soap, depending on the strength of the oils used (2 T. is equal to one ounce of oil). True essential oils tend to be stronger and you will probably only need from 1.25 to 3 oz. of essential oil for an 8 pound batch (another rule of thumb is 1-

2 tsp. essential oil per pound of soap).The **strongest common essential oils** are peppermint, rosemary, cinnamon, clove, spearmint and bitter almond. I probably left some out, but those are the ones you will use less of. Take a look at the chart below; the first three are essential oils while the others are fragrance oils. It's really up to your nose how much or little of an oil or fragrance you choose to use. This is just a guideline of how to use Essential and Fragrance oils.

Average Essential Oil	.7 oz. per pound of oils used in soap
Strong Essential Oil (like cinnamon, clove, mint, etc.)	.4 oz. per pound
Citrus Essential Oils	.9 oz. per pound
Average Fragrance Oil	.5 oz. (1 T./Tablespoon) per

	pound
Strong Fragrance Oil	1 - 1.5 tsp. per pound

Here are some helpful equivalents. Keep in mind that drop sizes can vary with the dropper.

88 Drops = 1 Teaspoon
3 Teaspoons = 1 Tablespoon
1 Tablespoon = 1/2 Ounce
2 Tablespoons = 1 Ounce
16 Tablespoons = 1 Cup
1 Cup = 8 Fluid Ounces

1 Tablespoon = 15 milliliters
1 Teaspoon = 5 milliliters
1/2 Teaspoon = 2.5 milliliters
1/4 Teaspoon = 1.25 milliliters
16 Drams = 1 Ounce
16 Ounces = 1 Pound

You can also create blended oil yourself. Take a coffee filter; fold it twice in half so you have a nice pointed end. Next take the oils you wish to blend and a dropper. Try 3 drops of one, 2 drops of another, and one final drop of another. Now place the coffee filter in a jar. Close the top and leave it there for a couple of days. Check to see if you like it. You can always adjust the drops and leave it again to make sure you like it. Write all the amounts and type of oils you use down as you do it, so you know your combination blend.

Coloring Your Soap

Soapers use various things to achieve colors for their soaps. Some soapers use candle color which works very well with soap when mixed into the fats before the lye solution is added. If you use bees wax as your fat, melt it first and use the color in the first few tablespoons of melted bees wax. You then pour in the rest of the bees wax after the color is poured in with the first few tablespoons. You can find candle color at your local hobby or arts and crafting store or online with a candle making supplies site.

Some people use crayons to color their soap but it takes more time and the colors are rather dilute. If you use crayons it is recommended that you use 1 to 3 regular crayons depending on the size of the recipes you are doing and how strong a color you want for your soap. People generally have to experiment with the crayons. From experienced soapers who have used crayons; they say that CERULEAN blue, yellow, orange, neon pink (from the neon box) brown, black and white work well so you would mix your colors from these as a possibility.

Any color made with Cerulean blue is great. The blue-greens, teals, forest greens, jungle greens all work good or the Cerulean blue with a yellow for a bunch of green variations. Neon pink only works for pink however when added to Cerulean blue makes lavender.

Colors that don't do well for crayon color in soap are Prussian blue and red, purple, reds, violet reds, burgundies, navy, blue, midnight blue, green (yellow and Prussian blue are a no) anything red or blue in Crayola language doesn't work. Violets are out too. Some people have been known to get a nice pink from red crayons but it depends on the brand.

Liquid food colorings are not very effective when coloring soap and will tend to fade in storage. Liquid chlorophyll is supposed to be nice and also natural cosmetic colorants. Certain spices can be used for coloring, particularly Turmeric. It will look like pumpkin pie when first poured, but changes to a nice warm beige after the soap sets up. I don't use any more than 1/2 to 1 teaspoon per batch. Here are some other suggestions; you can use up to 1/2 teaspoon per pound of soap if you like, depending on your desired shade.

Mix the powder into a bit of the soap and then mix that back in to the rest of the batch. Here are the colors:

Cayenne Pepper - Salmon color
Cinnamon Powder - Beige
Cocoa Powder - Coffee to Brown color
Curry Powder - Yellow Peach
Cinnamon Powder - Beige
Cocoa Powder - Coffee to Brown color
Curry Powder - Yellow Peach
Paprika - Peach
Turmeric - Golden Yellow
Dark squares of Cooking Chocolate - Brown
Liquid Chlorophyll - Light Green

Here are some soapers first hand experiences with natural substances. From Rachael: "I have good luck with yellows, gold's, tans, browns, oranges, greens, yellow-greens, pinks, salmons, greys and whites. I have no luck with natural purples, or blues. The powders can be mixed into the raw soap, into the lye water when hot, infused into the oils and strained, or mixed into a portion of the raw soap, and swirled into the rest of the soap, for designs. They vary from leaving pinpoint color dots throughout the whole block of soap, to simply staining the whole block of soap, to dramatic swirls that can look awesome. Start with a teaspoon to a pound of fats; a lot of them are mixed to achieve a certain range of color. The **reds-pinks-reddish tans-salmons** are cinnamon, paprika, some ground rose petals (some go brown), pink clays. The **yellows and gold's-to tans** are milk soaps (nonfat milk instead of water), turmeric, calendula, peanut oil soap, olive oil soap, beta carotene is tiny amounts. The **tans-browns** slippery elm (which I love because it smells sweet and agreeable), cocoa powder (which will have a dirty lather, but an awesome color, and cocoa butter soap just aches to have cocoa added to it), a lot of the ground roses and dried flowers turn brown, cloves. The **greens** are baby food spinach (strained) gives a clear celery green, chlorophyll from grass clippings, seaweed, sage, green clays. The **white** is titanium dioxide, it's all natural, just doesn't sound like it. **Orange** is baby food (pureed) carrots, beta carotene in small amounts, milk soap in high temperature range (with whole fat, not non-fat, cow's milk)."

From Sandy: "I ordered some **purple soap color** from cranberrylane.com out of Coquitlam, B.C. I got the ground rattan jot which is from an East Indian herb (I think), and a liquid form called "passion for purple" which is probably made by infusing oils with the ground rattan jot. I use 1 T. of liquid and 1/8 tsp. of ground in a 1 lb. batch. It gives a pale purple with purple speckles. Then I add passionflower FO and call it purple passion."

From Cindy: "I use alkanet root for **purple**, it will go from rosy purple to blue-purple depending on the ph of your mixture. You soak your main oil in it, I add one cup alkanet root to two cups olive oil, heat gently for a minute, then let sit for a few hours, then strain and incorporate in total weight of olive oil before adding lye. It will look bright red until the lye hits it! "

If you want natural sources of green in your soap (I'm talking "flecks" or pieces for texture), I'm told that dried parsley flakes and dried dill weed do a good job of holding up in soap and not turning brown. Fennel might work also (closely related to dill). Some folks like pieces of seaweed, and it smells pretty.

Chapter 9: Soap Recipes For Beginners

Now that you have a basic idea of the process involved in making soap; here are some basic recipes to start you off.

EASY COLD PROCESS SOAP 1

This is an easy, mild olive oil soap, good for beginners. This recipe makes 8 pounds of soap

Ingredients:

24 oz. olive oil

24 oz. coconut oil
38 oz. vegetable shortening (Crisco)
12 oz. lye
32 oz. distilled water
3-4 oz. any essential or fragrance oil

Equipment:

- Scale that weighs in pounds and ounces
- Large one-gal. stainless steel or enamel pot (use this exclusively for soap-making)
- Two plastic pitchers, 2-3 qt. size.
- Hand stick blender (optional, but makes tracing much easier)
- Plastic measuring cup 2-3 cup size
- Two wooden or plastic spoons (one for the lye and one for the oils. Use these exclusively for soap-making)
- Two kitchen thermometers (one for the lye and one for the oils - must read to over 100 degrees)
- Rubber gloves

- Safety goggles
- Clear plastic container with snap on lid 8" x 11" x 3" deep, or wooden soap mold lined with freezer paper
- Large piece of cardboard the size of the wooden mold - used as a lid
- Old blanket
- Freezer paper or plastic garbage bags

How to make the Soap:

Remember: Be sure to allow for the weight of the containers. Lye (Sodium Hydroxide NaOH) All ingredients should be weighed.

Begin by putting on your goggles and rubber gloves and weigh out 12 oz. of lye into one of the plastic containers. Weigh out 32 oz. of distilled water into the other container. Slowly and in a steady stream pour the lye into the water, stirring until dissolved. Do this in a well-ventilated area and try not to splash. Let the lye/water mixture sit until the temperature reaches between 100-125 degrees (unless otherwise stated by the recipe you are using). This may take several hours, but if you're in a hurry you can place the container in a cold water bath to bring down the temperature quicker.

In the meantime, get your oils ready by weighing out 24 oz. of coconut oil and 38 oz. of vegetable shortening and placing them into your pot. Heat them up just until they melt and then remove from heat and add the 24 oz. of olive oil. Stir to incorporate and put one of the thermometers into the pot to check the temperature. The oils will also have to be between 100-125 degrees (unless otherwise stated by the recipe you are using). Both the lye/water mixture and the oils will have to be at the same temperature before incorporating them.

Prepare your additives. Start with just 3-4 oz. of essential oil or a combination of essential oils (blend). *Note- (some essential oil scents are stronger, so use less, some are lighter and you may add more depending on your preference). Also, measure 1/4 cup of any dried herbs or flowers (optional). It's best to start simple for your first batch. You can also add 1-3 tablespoons of pigment (optional) for coloring; pre-disperse in a little liquid glycerin.

Line the mold container that you're using with a piece of freezer paper for easy release. If you are using our wooden soap mold, line it with freezer paper. Instructions on how to line a soap mold can be found at: *http://www.pvsoap.com/step_by_step instructions_ for_li.html.*

Check the temperature of the lye and oils. When it reaches between 100-125°, it's time to "make soap." Slowly pour the lye/water mixture into the oils, stirring continuously. You may continue to stir using a spoon or switch to the stick blender. Stir or blend in all the lye and you will begin to see the mixture thicken. Just as the mixture thickens to the point where you see tracks or "trace" in the soap, add essential oils and any dried ingredients or colorants. For swirling color, remove about 2 cups of the mixture and add the colorant to the 2 cups. Then add that back into the mold and swirl. Continue to stir or blend until you see designs on the top of the soap (this is known as tracing and can happen in 10-20 minutes depending on the temperature of your mixture). Quickly add the mixture to the mold. Cover with the lid. *Note* if the soap mixture does not fill the mold to the top, place a piece of freezer paper on top of the soap and then put the lid or a piece of cardboard on the container. This will prevent soda ash. Wrap in blankets and place in an undisturbed area for 18 hrs. Remove the blankets and lid and let the soap air in the mold for another few hours.

You should have a nice hard block of fresh soap which you can now remove from the mold. Let the block of soap sit for a day to firm up or slice into bars or chunks immediately. Then place bars in an open box or drying rack for 2 weeks or longer. Don't allow the bars to touch one another. The soap should be cured completely after 2 weeks, but the longer it cures, the milder and harder it will be.

COLD PROCESS SOAP BASE RECIPE VARIATION 2

This base recipe creates a mild, great lathering and firm bar of soap. It is my personal favorite. Recipe may be cut in half. Makes 12 lb. batch. Use wood or plastic mold (lined).

Ingredients:

- 3 lbs. distilled water
- 17 oz. lye (sodium hydroxide)

- 4 lbs. olive oil
- 2 lbs., 8 oz. coconut oil
- 1 lb., 8 oz. palm oil
- 1 oz. grapefruit seed extract (optional)
- 4-6 oz. of essential or fragrance oil

Temperature 90°-110° - 4 week cure time

To Super fat: add 3.2 oz. of Shea butter to the oils.

To Make An Oatmeal/Honey Soap:

Ingredients:

- At saponification add --1 cup ground oats and 4 tbsp. slightly warm honey,
- 4-6 oz. fragrance or essential oils (optional)

Follow the same basic instructions from the previous recipe

Same recipe but for a 2.5 lb. batch:

- 9 oz. distilled water
- 4-6 oz. lye (sodium hydroxide)
- 16 oz. olive oil

- 10 oz. coconut oil (76°)
- 6 oz. palm oil

ANOTHER COLD PRESS SOAP 3 (FAIRLY EASY)

A quick and easy cold process soap recipe that requires exactly 20 ounces of lye (the size of 1 canister from Certified Lye™) and yields a superior bar of natural soap

Ingredients:

- 41 oz. coconut oil (76°)
- 47 oz. olive oil
- 47 oz. palm oil
- 20 oz. lye (exactly 1 canister from Certified Lye™)
- 47 oz. water

This soap recipe makes a fabulous natural soap that is approximately 30% coconut oil, 35% olive oil, and 35% palm oil. The lye is discounted to 96%, so 4% of the oils will freely remain unsaponified in the soap. Because Certified Lye™ guarantees the accuracy of the net weight of lye in each canister, there is no need to measure or excessively handle the lye when using this recipe; it simply requires one canister of lye. The combined weight of the ingredients is 202 ounces, which requires a soap pot with an 8-quart capacity to allow extra room for stirring. This soap recipe makes approximately 40 regular size bars of soap. When making this soap recipe, all proper safety precautions and soap making procedures should be followed.

MILK SOAPS

Cold Process Goat Milk Soap

Goat's milk soap has a creamy smooth texture and is very nourishing for your skin.

Makes 4 lbs. Weigh all ingredients, following basic cold process method.

Ingredients:

- 16 oz. goat milk (frozen/slushy)
- 6.5 oz. lye (sodium hydroxide)
- 8 oz. palm oil
- 17 oz. coconut oil (76°)
- 17 oz. olive oil
- 1 oz. grapefruit seed extract
- 2-3 oz. essential oil

NOTE: You can also use half goat milk and half distilled water.

Spiced Milk and Honey Soap

* Milk and honey both can cause *overheating* in soap. When you make a recipe with milk or honey or both, you should **only slightly insulate, or not at all.** With a deep mold, I think I would completely pass on insulating. If you are sure the soap is at thick trace when you pour and don't insulate... hopefully, you won't get a separation.

Ingredients:

- 48 oz. shortening (Crisco type - 3# can)
- 22 oz. coconut oil
- 16 oz. olive oil
- 24 oz. cold water
- 12 oz. lye crystals

Temperature: around 100 degrees

After incorporating the lye solution with the oils, add:

- 12 oz. can evaporated milk, warmed (for lighter colored soap with firmer texture, you can use only 6 oz. evaporated milk and increase the water by 2-4 ounces)
- 1/4 cup honey, dissolved into milk (for a lighter color and less tendency to separate, you can cut this back to 1 T.)

At light trace, mix in:

- 3/4 oz. cinnamon oil
- 1/2 oz. clove oil

The essential oils will accelerate trace, so be prepared to quickly pour the soap when it starts to thicken. The milk will turn colors as you watch, after being added. Maybe if it had been cooler, it wouldn't have gotten quite so dark, but the color goes well with the spices. In the future, I will not insulate a batch like this until it begins to cool after going through the "gel" stage. Rachael had a different method for mixing her milk soap (on the Soaps Using Animal Fats page) and you might prefer to do it that way. Other people have used this method and it has worked fine. It will take longer to cure than some of the other batches, partly because of the extra water added during the re-melt and because of the milk content. Probably only a matter of a couple of weeks more.

Milky Rose Soap Bar

Ingredients:

- 1/4 cup freshly picked or dried rose petals, the more fragrant the better

- 16 oz. clear M&P soap base
- 1/8th cup goats milk, may use buttermilk or other milk of choice
- 1/2-1 tsp. rose petals fragrance oil

Equipment:

- glass measuring cup
- metal spoon
- mold of your choice
- microwave
- alcohol in spray bottle

Instructions:

Add 16oz (1 cup) of clear M&P soap base (or any clear soap base) into your measuring cup. Melt your soap in the microwave at 10-20 sec intervals, stirring between each time, do not allow to boil. Add your rose petals and stir well. The hot soap will help "steep" the petals and allow them to release their beneficial properties. Add your milk and stir well. If the milk causes your soap to cool too much after adding, forming a skin on your base, place back in microwave for 5-10 seconds. Add fragrance oil, stir well and pour into your molds. Spritz on your alcohol and allow soap to set up, approximately 30-40 minutes.

*Package in cello bags with a few faux rose petals for a very nice look.

Vitamin Soap

Ingredients:

Lye Solution:

- 3 lbs (48 oz.) distilled water
- 475g sodium hydroxide

Fats:

- 2 1/2 lbs (40 oz.) coconut oil
- 1 1/2 lbs (24 oz.) palm oil
- 1 3/4 lbs (28 oz.) olive oil, Grade B or pomace (2 lbs less 1/2 cup)
- 1 oz. (2 tbsp.) wheat germ oil
- 1 oz. (2 tbsp.) carrot seed oil
- 1 oz. (2 tbsp.) carrot root oil

- 1 oz. (2 tbsp.) vitamin e oil
- 1/2 lb. (8 oz.) sweet almond oil
- 1/2 lb. (8 oz.) apricot kernel oil
- 1/2 lb. (8 oz.) kukui nut oil
- 1/2 lb. (8 oz.) jojoba oil
- 4 oz. shea butter
- 30g grapefruit seed extract

Nutrients:

- 2 oz. (4 tbsp.) avocado oil
- 2 oz. (4 tbsp.) evening primrose oil, borage oil or rosa mosqueta rosehip seed oil

Scent:

- 45-50g (about 3 oz.) essential oils

Instructions:

Add lye to water and let cool to 80 degrees. Melt fats and let cool to 80-90 degrees. Add lye to fats and stir briskly for up to one hour until it "traces". Add nutrients and essential oils, stir to combine and pour into molds. Cover with blankets and allow it to sit for 24 to 48 hours until it stops generating heat. When hard (up to a week), cut and remove from mold. Set out to dry and cure for 4-6 weeks.

Baby Soap

Ingredients:

- 194 g lye
- 19 oz. water
- 8 oz. sweet almond oil
- 7 oz. jojoba
- 2 oz. castor
- 4 oz. shea butter
- 19 oz. coconut oil
- 14 oz. palm oil
- 1 oz. vitamin E oil

Instructions:

Heat oils to 100 degrees. Combine lye and water and cool to 100 degrees. Combine oils and lye/water mixing well. At trace add the vitamin E oil. Pour into a mold and proceed as you would with cold process soap.

HOT PROCESS SOAP/OVEN HOT PROCESS

In hot process soap you put the soap in the oven and leave it there according to the recipe

Ingredients:

- 18 oz. canola oil
- 8 oz. coconut oil
- 18 oz. olive oil
- 12 oz. distilled water
- 6 oz. lye
- 1 tbsp. apple pie spice
- 1 tbsp. turmeric
- 2 tbsp. apple FO

Instructions:

Make sure you know the safety precautions before making any soap. Preheat oven to 200 degrees. Add lye to water and cool to 100 degrees. Melt oils. Melt oils in the same pot that later you put in the oven. Cool to 100 degrees. Mix oils and lye water together using a stick blender. At light trace add spices then FO. Cover with a lid and put it in the oven for 1 1/2 hours. Scoop into the mold. After 24 hours, remove it from the mold and cut. I allow it several days to harden, then package.

Moisturizing Hot Process Soap

Use oven guidelines above to make this soap

Ingredients:

- 20 oz. palm oil
- 17 oz. coconut oil
- 16 oz. safflower oil
- 8 oz. olive oil
- 3 oz. sweet almond oil
- 24 oz. distilled water
- 9 oz. sodium hydroxide

Instructions:

Follow basic hot process soap instructions. You can add any essential oils, botanicals, clays or other additives at trace or just before pouring into molds.

Hot Process Emu Oil Soap

Ingredients:

- 16.8 oz. olive oil (28%)
- 12 oz. coconut oil (20%)
- 9 oz. palm oil (15%)
- 7.2 oz. emu oil (12%)
- 3.6 oz. castor oil (6%)
- 3 oz. avocado oil (5%)
- 2.4 oz. cocoa butter (4%)
- 2.4 oz. shea butter (4%)
- 1.2 oz. jojoba (2%)
- 1.2 oz. sweet almond oil (2%)
- 23 oz. distilled water
- 8.14 oz. lye (6% excess fat)

Fragrance and color optional

Instructions:

OBSERVE ALL STANDARD SAFETY

PROCEDURES. Weigh lye and water. Mix and set aside. Weigh and melt hard oils in microwave. Add to pre-warmed crock. Weigh and add liquid oils to crock. Add lye/water to crock oils while stirring gently. Bring to trace alternating between whisk and stick blender. Cover and cook until done. Glop into mold. Unmold and cut when cool.

Hand Milled Soap

Ingredients:

- 1 lb. soap (I use goat's milk)
- 1/8 cup distilled water
- 2 tbsp. fine ground chamomile
- 2 tbsp. ground lavender buds
- 1/8 cup emu oil (optional)
- 5 drops lavender essential oil
- 2 drops roman chamomile essential oil

Instructions:

In double boiler, slowly melt soap with water. When it reaches a jelly-like consistency; gently stir in herbs, emu oil and essential oils. Carefully pour into prepared molds. Wait 24 hours and remove from molds. Let cure for about 4 weeks. This is so gentle and relaxing it can be used on children.

Milled Mango Mint Shampoo Bar

Use this for hair

Ingredients:

- 1 cup grated soap
- 1/2 cup water
- 1/4 cup olive oil
- 1/4 cup castor oil
- 1 T dried crushed peppermint leaves
- 15 drops mango fragrance oil

Instructions:

Melt soap and water in heat resistant glass bowl in a saucepan. When soap is stringy add the remaining ingredients. Pour into prepared molds or hand molds. Let them cool for at least 2 hours before removing them from molds. Allow them to cure for at least a week prior to use.

MELT AND POUR SOAPS

Buttercream Facial Bar

Ingredients:

- 4 oz goats milk M&P base
- 1 tbsp. powdered whole milk
- 1/2 tsp. of hydrolyzed silk amino acid
- 8 drops of buttercream FO
- 8 drops of vanilla FO ac

Instructions:

Gently melt the soap base over a double boiler until liquefied and then allow it to cool slightly. Stir in the powdered milk and silk amino acid. Lastly, add fragrance oils and pour into a soap mold of your choice. This is an excellent face and body bar. ENJOY!

Chocolate Chip Cookie Soap Recipe

This soap looks like a cookie. These turn

out very well!

Ingredients:

- 1 lb. white or clear coconut M&P base
- Cocoa powder or brown pigment
- 1 lb. cocoa butter
- 1 T chocolate FO
- Small round soap molds

Instructions:

Melt the cocoa butter with most of the white or clear base, leaving a little behind. I use white and add a little cocoa powder to it to get it a very soft brown.

Keep melted, although you can allow it to cool slightly. As it does add the chocolate FO. Melt the leftover soap quickly and add a dark brown dye or a good amount of cocoa powder to make it a much deeper color than the first batch.

Lay this soap (the dark batch) out over a wax paper lined plate to become tacky. When the soap has become harder (this is a small amount of soap and does not take long), pick off a few chunks (these will be your chips) and line them at the bottom of the soap molds.

Spritz very lightly with alcohol if desired.

Now add the cooled but semi liquid big batch over the hard chips.

Let it sit for a few minutes to continue forming skin.

After the top layer of skin is formed (the soap showing from the mold), add some more of the leftover chips to this part to make the cookie appear as it has chips all over. You can also drop a chip or two in to blend in and be more natural appearing when combining the soaps.

The cocoa butter gives the soap its own scent, as does the cocoa powder, and it looks just like a little wax cookie. The lather is bubbly brown and very luxurious!

Chocolate Lovers Exfoliating Soap Ingredients

Ingredients:

- 2 lb. M&P soap base
- 1/2 cup goat's milk powder
- 1 tsp. powdered kola nut (or other brown herb)
- 1 tsp. macadamia nut oil
- 1/2 tsp. cocoa butter
- 1/2 tsp. mango butter
- 1/2 tsp. silk amino acids
- Chocolate fragrance oil

Instructions:

Melt the butters and glycerin soap gently over a double boiler. When liquid, blend in macadamia oil and silk. Let it cool slightly. Pour about 1 cup of soap into a separate dish and blend very well with Goat's Milk powder, making sure to eliminate all lumps. Combine with rest of melted soap, mix in fragrance oil and Kola Nut Powder to achieve desired chocolaty color and scent. Pour into molds.

Coffee and Cream Soap

This one is used to help fight cellulite.

Ingredients:

- 8 oz. coconut opaque M&P base
- 2 tsp. lanolin
- 2 tsp. aloe vera gel
- 3 tsp. coffee grounds
- 2 tsp. heavy whipping cream
- 10 drops coffee fragrance oil
- 10 drops vanilla fragrance oil

Instructions:

Melt the soap base in a double boiler. Add all the other ingredients and stir well. Pour into molds and let it sit for 3 hours Put molds in freezer for 5 minutes and pop them out.

Honey Bee Soap Ingredients:

Ingredients:

- 4 oz. honey melt & pour soap
- 1 tbsp. beeswax
- 1 tbsp. honey
- Dash of bee pollen (optional)

Instructions:

This soap is simple but beautiful and delightful! The color comes out looking like hard honey - it's a golden, gorgeous shade that looks very nice and professional. The bee pollen, honey, and beeswax are all wonderful for the skin. Melt the soap base in a double boiler. As the soap is melting, add the honey and wax. Allow the melted soap to cool and form a film. Sprinkle in some bee pollen if so desired. Give a brief stir and pour into a delicate mold - heart shape, a bee soap mold, or any other creative mold. Leave to harden for many hours, possibly overnight, and enjoy in the morning!

Makes a hard, dependable bar that smells like honey.

Relaxing Lavender and Green Tea Soap

Ingredients:

- 1 lb. M&P goats milk soap
- 2 tsp. beeswax (omit for a softer bar)
- 1 tbsp. solid coconut oil
- 2 tbsp. powdered green tea (grind in a coffee grinder)
- 2 tbsp. lavender powder
- 1/2 tsp. lavender fragrance oil
- 1/4 tsp. cucumber fragrance oil
- 1/4 tsp. bergamot fragrance oil
- 5 drops green tea fragrance oil
- Optional: soap coloring green and purple

Instructions:

Melt soap base, coconut oil and beeswax in a double boiler. When completely melted, remove from heat and add powdered lavender & green tea and the fragrance oils. Pour into molds and let solidify. Green tea is used for reflection and enlightenment and lavender and cucumber are used to soothe and relax.

Tip: Get creative! Separate the melted ingredients and add the green tea to one half and the lavender to the other. I color the lavender with purple soap color (red and blue soap dye) and green tea side with a couple drops green. You can cut the scent in half and put it in each side.

Herbal Soap Scrolls

This one can make a beautiful presentation for gifts

Ingredients:

- 8 oz. clear M&P base
- 1/4 cup herbs (I use orange peel, lavender, mint, or oatmeal)
- Fragrance

Instructions:

Melt M&P according to directions. Add color and scent as desired. Pour liquid soap onto a 9x13 cookie sheet, and then sprinkle desired herbs on top. While still pliable, (not liquid or fully firm) carefully peel up one edge of the soap "sheet" and gently pull soap from cookie sheet. While still warm, roll the soap into a "scroll" and tie with raffia at both ends and in the middle. Shrink wrap to prevent any unraveling. Instruct users to simply slice off an end of the soap to use in each bath.

Sweet Heart Soaps

Ingredients:

- 1 oz. heart shaped chocolate mold
- 4 oz. round soap mold
- 1 oz. M&P soap (clear or white)
- 3 drops clove oil
- 2 drops cinnamon oil
- 2 drops buttercream fragrance

- FDC dye for deep red or burgundy coloring
- 3 oz. clear M&P soap
- 2 drops buttercream fragrance

Instructions:

Melt 1 oz. of soap. Add essential oils and 2 drops buttercream and color to a deep red. Pour into heart shape mold and place in freezer. Let it freeze for 30-45 minutes.

Then melt 3 oz. clear soap. Add the 2 drops buttercream. Remove the heart soap from freezer and unmold. Pour very small amount of melted clear soap into the round mold. Place the heart into mold. Cover with the remainder of melted soap.

Allow the soap to harden. When set, approx. 1-2 hours, unmold.

*This soap is great for baskets and gifts around Valentine's Day.

Body Soap that Exfoliates and Moistures

Ingredients:

- 8 oz. shea or cocoa butter M&P soap base
- 2 tbsp. shea butter
- 1 tbsp. cocoa butter
- 2 tbsp. finely ground oatmeal
- 1 tbsp. rose petal powder
- 20 drops red colorant
- 40 drops rose geranium essential oil
- 20 drops ylang-ylang essential oil

Instructions:

Melt the soap base over a double boiler. Add the Shea butter and cocoa butter and heat until melted. Add the oatmeal and rose petal powder. Add the red colorant and continue stirring, making sure it is fully incorporated. Lastly, add the essential oils and stir well. Pour into desired soap molds and let set. Note: After the soaps have started to set and are no longer in danger of spilling over the mold, put the molds into the freezer for 10 to 15 minutes. The soaps will pop out of the molds very easily!

Moisturizing Earth Soap

Ingredients:

- 1 lb. any M&P soap base
- 1/4 cup clay of choice (I use Moroccan red & kaolin)
- 2 tbsp. lanolin
- 1 tbsp. high oleic sunflower seed oil
- 1 tbsp. vitamin E, 1000 IU oil
- 4 drops mandarin essential oil
- 3 drops Spanish lemon essential oil

Instructions:

Melt soap base and lanolin together. Completely blend in all oils. If using more than one type of clay, separate soap into equal portions and blend one type into each portion, making sure to get all clumps. Pour into molds, allow to harden. If using more than one color of clay, pour first type into mold, allow to cool until slightly thicker but still liquid, then pour other type to fill.

Tea Rose Beauty Facial Bar With Anti-Bacterial Properties

Ingredients:

- 4 oz. M&P soap base
- 10 drops rose E.O.
- 5 drops tea tree oil
- 1/2 tsp. jojoba oil
- Red color

Instructions:

Melt base. Add rose E.O. and tea tree oil. Mix slowly to not cause any bubbles to form. Add jojoba oil and color, mix again. Pour into mold. Remove when set.

Tea Tree and Kelp Healing Soap

Ingredients:

- 1 lb. suspension M&P base
- 2 tbsp. kelp powder

- 2 tbsp. flax seed meal
- 15-20 drops tea tree essential oil

Instructions:

Melt the soap base over a double boiler. Remove a small amount of soap into a cup. Mix kelp and flax meal into this, then add back into the rest of the melted soap base. Add the Tea Tree oil last. Tea Tree and Kelp are both very strong smelling, so they help to 'hide' each other. Kelp is a great skin detoxifier, and Tea Tree has tons of good properties, such as being an anti-fungal and healing aid. Milled Flax seeds are a nice gentle exfoliator. This is my most popular soap. Try using a Goat's Milk M&P base if you find this too drying.

Vanilla Honey Oatmeal Recipe

Ingredients:

- 2lbs. of clear or white M&P soap
- 1/8 to 1/4 cup of Honey

- 3/4 cup of ground oatmeal
- 1 tsp. of vitamin E
- 1 tbsp. of vanilla oil
- 1 tbsp. of frankincense and myrrh oil (fragrance oil or essential oil)

Instructions:

Cut the M&P into chunks and heat on a double boiler. Add honey and vitamin E. Let your base cool approx. 5-10 min or until it starts to form a skin on top, stir the skin back into the base. When the base starts to thicken slightly add your fragrance and oatmeal. You want your oatmeal to be suspended in your base. Pour into molds. Use a loaf pan. Let it sit and harden for several hours and unmold. Slice and let it sit for 24hr and wrap with plastic wrap.

French Citrus Bar (great for oily skin)

Ingredients:

- 8 oz. M&P (clear or opaque)

- 1 tsp. french green clay
- 1/2 tsp. lemon peel powder
- 1/2 tsp. orange peel powder
- 1 tsp. jojoba oil
- 5 drops tea tree essential oil
- 5 drops lemon essential oil
- 2 drops lemongrass essential oil

Instructions:

Cut up the M&P soap into small chunks and gently melt in the microwave or in a double-boiler. Add the clay, citrus powders and the jojoba oil and stir thoroughly. Add essential oils and stir again. Pour into molds. Makes about 2 to 3 bars. The clay and citrus powders draw off the oils in your face; the essential oils are antibacterial. If you have only slightly oily skin, you may want to use a light moisturizer afterwards.

Chapter 10: Conclusion

This little book is a great introduction on how to start you off making your own soap. Making homemade soap is an enjoyable and creative experience. You can get as innovative as you want with the ingredients you use once you get the hang of how the soap process goes. The only way to become an experienced "soaper" is by trial and error. Get busy and get started gathering your equipment and supplies so you can begin your personal journey on becoming the best soap maker ever.

Meet the Author

Ten years ago Janet Brooks took a soap making class with some friends and the rest is history. Janet now has a spare bedroom dedicated to her soap passion and enjoys making, using and selling her special blend soaps.

Janet originally enjoyed giving her homemade soaps to friends and family for holidays and special occasions. With the encouragement of her daughter, Janet began to sell her special blends at local craft fairs and was overwhelmed at the popularity of her soaps.

Janet and her husband Jack reside in Oregon and are owned by four black labs. When Janet is not brewing up a new soap batch she enjoys reading, quilting and spending time with her grandkids.

www.ingramcontent.com/pod-product-compliance
Lightning Source LLC
LaVergne TN
LVHW021942060526
838200LV00042B/1901